Elemental Endeavors
Book 2:

water

T. Jason Vanderlaan

BALM AND BLADE
PUBLISHING

ISBN: 978-0-9841386-4-7

Published by Balm and Blade Publishing
1475 Hollow Road
Birchrunville, PA 19421
www.balmandblade.com

Author photo by Matthew White

Cover design by T. Jason Vanderlaan
www.jasonvanderlaan.com

~ Dedicated to Dave and Mama ~

I love you both!

Contents

Introduction

We seem to experience life in cycles: calm seas followed by raging storms. We all long for the peaceful stages of life, while we look with apprehension towards the turbulent times. But are tranquil waters always good? Are rough waves always bad? And how do we make sense of these cycles that seem to happen at random, both in their frequency and intensity?

Whether I am simply discouraged by circumstances or devastated by tragedy, it can be hard to see beyond the current moment. I want to know that this isn't where the story ends. I want to know that there is more than this repetition, more than continually returning to the confinement of meaningless doldrums or the captivity of endless heartache. I want to know that there is more to life than this.

What if we could know that our story doesn't end in the middle? Wouldn't it be easier to weather the storms if we knew that they had a purpose, mysterious as it might be? What if we could know that at the end of it all, there would be something good?

Whether we are wandering aimlessly across the ocean or searching for some distant shoreline, we wonder if there is a purpose to all we go through. We want to know that our pain isn't wasted.

Would it change anything if we knew that there was an unseen hand guiding us through our journey, giving us both calm and chaos? What if we had someone to lead us beside still waters as well as take us through the valley of the shadow of death? Or, at the very least, what if there is a way to become stronger instead of torn down by whatever fate throws at us?

I don't have all the answers, but I know this:

You are not alone.

Your suffering is not meaningless.

There is more than this.

There is hope.

Take heart.

T. Jason Vanderlaan

To Kiss the Sea

The sun came down
to kiss the sea,
and sent a pink-purple blush
across the dimming sky.

The ripples of their romance
came bounding on the waves,
splashed upon the shore,
and then went back for more.

I wrote poetry in the sand,
and counted myself blessed
to have witnessed such love.

The Call

Chest deep, I feel
the salty water slide past
to grace the edges of dry sand,
then return to the depths.

Your tidal heart is calling:
Come and I will draw you in,
even into My very heart.

T. Jason Vanderlaan

Venture
(To the tune of Franz Schubert's *Serenade*)

Standing on the docks,
a salt breeze swirls through my hair,
across my skin, into each pore,
claiming every part of me –
pulling me towards the sea.

But I need no persuasion.

This is what I was born for:
a journey across restless waves,
risking everything for the chance
that on a distant shore
I'll find all I've ever wanted.

I've charted my course,
mapped my destination,
and I know
as sure as the stars shine at night,
this is what I want.

I'm ready.

Water

T. Jason Vanderlaan

Soul Saturation

A single sleek sailboat
slides across the surface
of the salty summer sea,
sending signals of solitude
to the shore on which I stand.
Silently, I seek serenity
in the sublime saturation
of my Savior's sufficiency.

Summer Storms I

Remember the time at the Fourth of July party when you told me you loved me? A summer storm was building in the distance, slowly making its way towards us. I was standing by the railing of the back porch, watching lighting flash on the horizon. I was so engrossed by the storm that I jumped with surprise when you touched my arm.

You blushed when you told me your feelings. It broke my heart to tell you I didn't feel the same. You were one of my best friends and it tore me apart to hurt you like that. I wrote a poem the next day entitled *The Handle Cuts Like the Blade*, though I think now that I was probably being a bit naïve. Still, I hated myself for being unable to love you back.

Two years later, I came home for summer break and everything was different. I drove over to your house to catch up on all the news and reminisce about old times. We went walking in the woods behind your house. You had changed so much. Or maybe I had. Whatever it was, your smile melted my heart like I never thought a smile could.

We got caught in a downpour on our way back. I remember so clearly the sound of your laughter mixing beautifully with the rain on the leaves. Your wet hair stuck to your forehead and neck. Your eyes sparkled with excitement.

We dashed under the weeping willow in front of your house. I took your hand in mine and when you didn't pull away I leaned in and kissed you. I'd never seen you so happy before. And I was happy to finally be able to return your love. It's a mystery, really, how things turn around when we least expect them to. Especially when they turn so beautifully.

A Pebble

What is this pebble
that has plopped
into my perfect pool
of peaceful ponderings?

What is this stone
that has shaken
the still surface
of my sheltered serenity?

Reverberating ripples
rush through my heart,
reminding me:
it only takes a pebble.

Turbulent tremors
thrash through my thoughts,
telling me:
it only takes a stone.

And in a single moment
everything can change.

Across These Waters

We want perfection,
smooth and slender,
sleek as a knife's edge.

We search,
scouring the shore
for the destined one –
perhaps buried, perhaps
lying in plain sight.

At last, our fingers find, grasp,
discover texture and weight.

And then:
grip,
pull back,
and fling across these waters.

But with each skip
our hearts beat a broken rhythm
as we realize what we've lost.

T. Jason Vanderlaan

Puzzle Piece

Every time I find where I belong
the shape changes
and I'm out of place again.

Summer Storms II

At least, I thought so at the time. I've never told you, but I always regretted our first kiss. I'm sure we both have a lot of regrets now, but that one haunts me the most. I took something from you that was not mine to take. I wanted so desperately to make you happy that I didn't consider whether or not I could make your happiness last.

A storm had passed over just before you came by to talk. The scent of rain was fresh as I sat there, listening to the sound of your words shattering my heart. It felt like a dream. A strange mix of certainty and confusion. You laid out my faults immaculately. I couldn't argue against such evidence. But I knew I loved you. And despite all our problems, I knew we were good together. But there you were, saying goodbye.

You kissed me on the cheek before leaving. As you drove down the road, I watched in stunned silence. But I didn't cry. Wouldn't let myself. Not because I thought crying was a wimpy thing to do. No, I didn't cry because to do so felt like admitting that it was over. That you were gone. That I had lost you. And I wasn't ready to do that yet. I was willing to wait for you as long as it took. And I did wait, praying something would change. Every time my phone rang I hoped it was you.

You never called.

An Unavoidable Casualty

A dry leaf
scrapes across
the cold sidewalk,
just before it crunches
beneath my foot.

Up ahead,
a lamppost flickers
and dies.

I walk past it
and continue in darkness.

A tear escapes from my eye
and rolls down my cheek,
making this chilly night
even colder.

There is no mercy
in these winter winds.

T. Jason Vanderlaan

Riptide (Fair Warning)

I.
The plot thickens
like my blood
as the temperature drops.

II.
No man is an island,
though I wish I were,
for even islands
can bring comfort to the shipwrecked.

There is nothing as lonely
as a lighthouse.

III.
The tension is beneath
And it's pulling me under.
This is over my head
And it's pushing me down.

IV.
It's on nights like tonight
that the ink runs dry.

Here, I give you
my last drop.

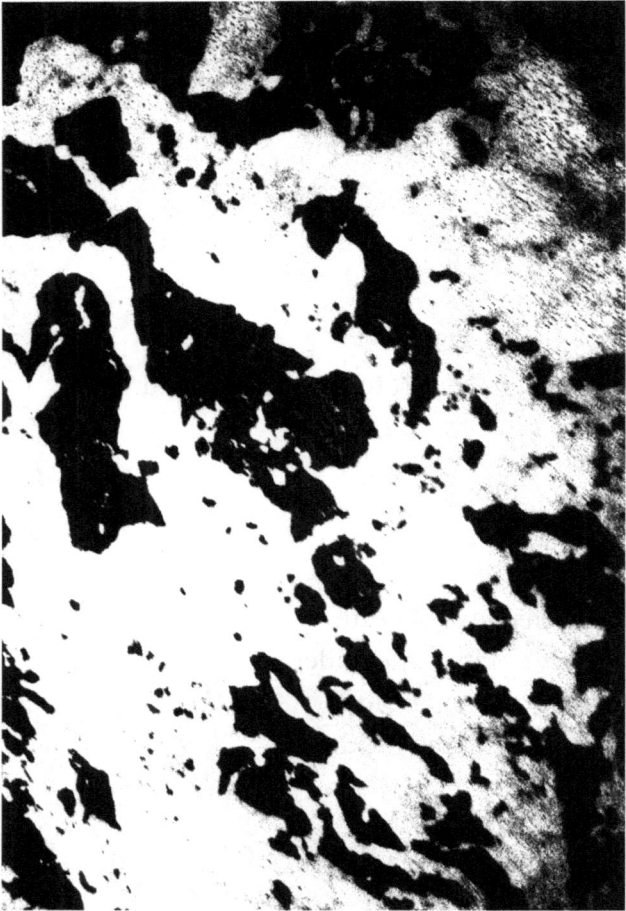

T. Jason Vanderlaan

Crumpled Pieces of Paper, Tossed on the Floor

I.
Nearly every step
    of every day
   I've ever lived
has been perfectly
      calculated.

I want
    need
escape.

II.
Justified, all my text
neatly in rows
      perfectly straight
on both sides

no longer.

III.
In the Ice House I
sit
   wishing I
could sing and dance

instead of
        brooding
over my overly self-serious
        poetry.

IV.
Inspired by
FUN!

    (Could it be so easy?)

I laugh at the thought.

  (I *laugh*?)

V.
Reckless, but
not in the let's-get-drunk-and-
        smoke-pot-and-
        have-sex
kind of way.

Nor even in the I-shouldn't-but-
        I-want-to
        way.

beenthere, donethat, wore
             the chains.

I want the exhilaration of
a risk well-taken
  not well-calculated.

VI.
Perhaps only a detour
           an excursion,
           a way to leave
           and come back
to myself.

But not
  myself.

VII.
Really, I don't know
           what I want:

maybe   nothing.

maybe everything.

Storm

(To the tune of Carl Orff's *O Fortuna*)

Forsaken, I am utterly
at the mercy of all I can't comprehend.

Our ship is the waves' plaything,
tossed about while the thunder
laughs and roars from above.

And still the sea winds call to me
but I am no longer willing
to accept their final invitation.

They beckon for my surrender.

And then: silence – the sea relaxes,
eases her anger, considers pity.

Perhaps there is still a way,
still a chance that I will find
the land I long for.

I hold my breath, hoping.

But then fate twists, flits crookedly
like lightning above
as the sky inhales,
deep and terrible,

and the brutal finale is unleashed
like Leviathan's tortured breath.

In Moments of Uncertainty

It is so easy
in moments of uncertainty
to doubt the sure words of God.

But we must not be
as a wave tossed in the wind.

When He tells us to hold on,
we must be strong
and never loosen our grip.

And when He tells us to surrender
we must dare to venture
all we've sought to hold.

Midnight

Lightning flashed across my mind
illuminating a landscape of thoughts,
and for the briefest of moments
I could see everything clearly
before the shroud of darkness returned.

T. Jason Vanderlaan

Forgotten Anniversary
(A Year After My Re-Baptism)

Airport lines and
forgotten memories.

My sister calls out:
Happy Anniversary!
I smile and nod, but
I had forgotten You.

I'm sorry.

I turn, check my bags, and
forget again.

Summer Storms III

I popped *Cast Away* into the DVD player without even thinking about it. I'd never really liked the movie that much, but that day it cut me to the core.

The love story didn't even match ours. But when Tom Hanks was on screen, talking about how it felt to lose the love of his life and how he just had to keep breathing and waiting to see what the tide would bring in, I just broke down and wept.

But what if nothing changes? What if you survive the sea only to be relegated to the living death of an aching, meaningless existence? What if hope is empty?

T. Jason Vanderlaan

Rose Petals, Rain Drops, and an Empty Hand

I never imagined
being so angry at you,
but this –
you have shattered me,
rendered me irreparable.

You have broken
your promise – never
to let go, never be apart.

I held your hand
one last time, but
it returned no warmth.

And they say
don't let the sun go down,
but you have gone down,
left me behind, left me
to stand alone –

hot tears falling
onto the unfeeling dirt
that now separates me
from you.

T. Jason Vanderlaan

Shipwrecked
(To the tune of Tomaso Albinoni / Remo
Giazotto's *Adagio in G Minor*)

Nothing but splinters remain,
shards of dreams that pierce the skin,
burrow in, infecting what's left of hope.

And still I crawl
across the rocky shore
where the waves deposited
my battered body.

Still I search
for others broken like me.

But still I fear
that there is no escape
from this desolate island.

We may find each other.
We may survive together.
But we are lost together.

The sun disappears
below the horizon,
taking with it
my hopes of rescue.

T. Jason Vanderlaan

Husband and Son: A Eulogy

Promises are broken today,
but not by choice,
as hopes take their last breath
along with this man.

There are some things
that should never be,
but they are unfolding
before my eyes.

Wedding photos arrive in the mail,
accompanied by sympathy cards;
she opens them alone.

A father buries his son
and a mother waters the grave
with her tears – no flowers grow.

Their hearts are breaking,
and I am broken with them.

Loss is Not Less, Even With This Hope

We do not mourn
like those without hope.

But we do mourn.

Because even with the promise
of a future free from separation,

We still have no cure
for the common cold
of this merciless Winter –
life frozen, barren, denied.

Our hearts were never meant to break.
We were never meant to be apart.

And though we know it is only temporary,
we still have nothing to fill the void.

T. Jason Vanderlaan

Dragon's Breath

We tremble beneath
the venomous gaze
of that ancient serpent
as his ever-thirsty fangs
seek to devour every joy.

And as the breath of his mouth
scorches every land,
he vows to never rest
until every garden is a desert.

But we know
there is a fire that will burn
even hotter
than the dragon's last breath,

turning his promises to ash
and his curses to dust
trampled beneath our feet.

And in the wake of his demise,
healing streams flow out to fill
the scars upon our earth.

Water

Summer Storms IV

I heard about the fire that consumed your home. What can I possibly say to bring you any comfort now? As you know, I'm not the best at dealing with the aftermath of heartbreak. But I am getting pretty good at one thing: breathing. And waiting out the tough times when things don't quite make sense. It's a mystery, really, how things turn around when we least expect it.

You know, they have some great storms up here in the mountains. I'm sure they've got some good ones where you are too, or wherever you're going next. That's the great thing about storms: there are good ones wherever you go. Especially in the summer.

And as strange as it sounds, they always bring me a sense of comfort. And hope. Because with every storm comes a chance for change. For better or worse, storms are catalysts. And while I've weathered my share of devastating storms, I know that even those can bring something good with them.

36

Then one day, someday, each of us will find a storm that we just can't bear to lose, and we'll run with it and never let it go. And it won't let us go. The rain will keep falling, drenching us to the core, and we'll just run even harder. The lightning will keep flashing to show us the way and the thunder will keep roaring to remind us that we're a part of something grand and majestic.

And when that day comes, it'll be like a dream. We won't understand it all, but we won't have to, because we'll be caught up in something so wonderful that all the imperfections and uncertainties of the moment will lose their meaning.

But unlike a dream, we won't wake up. We'll just keep running and laughing and loving, and the rain will keep falling in slow motion to the flash and boom of the storm. It'll be a mystery, but a beautiful one.

So keep breathing. And hoping. Because you never know when another summer storm might come your way.

T. Jason Vanderlaan

I Pretend Like I am Wise Enough to Write Proverbs

I.
Give me a moment
and I'll teach you
how to live.

But give me a lifetime
and I'll teach you
how to die.

II.
We praise happiness
and shun sadness,
but joy is deeper than both
and its depth can satisfy.

Five For Three To One

Five trite memories
eat away at the moon
with a passionate white fire,

for I cannot forget
the intensity of the red
we painted on the night sky

three years ago when
we discovered the diamond lake
and dove into its depths

to find a hidden teardrop
that longed to be delivered
from among the liquid conformity.

One day I will return,
with moon dust in my hair,
and add my sorrow to these gems.

T. Jason Vanderlaan

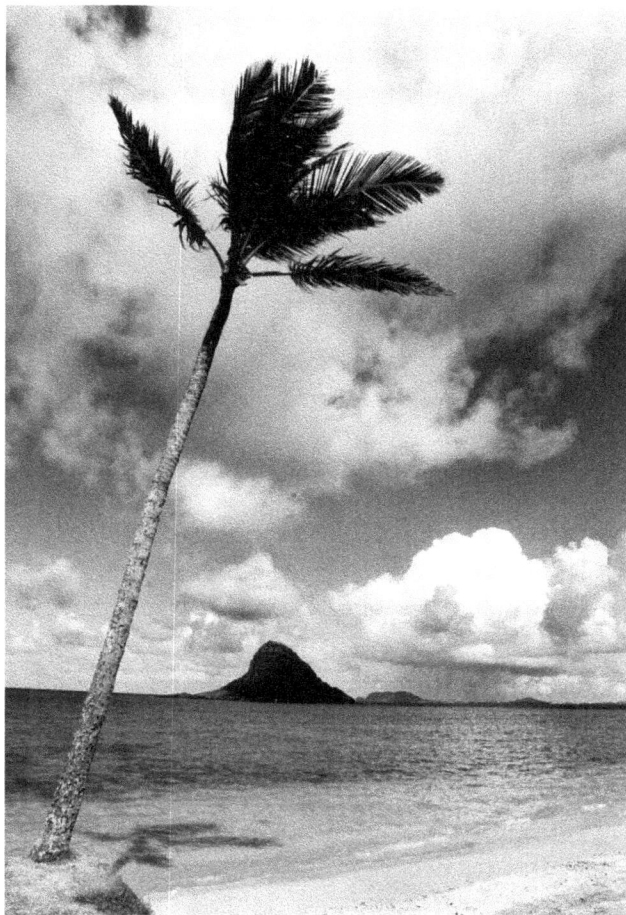

In the Air, On My Way Back From Hawaii

I think I would rather have
taken a boat back to the mainland.

There's just something about
this ten hour flight
that threatens to nullify
everything I've just experienced.

It just doesn't seem right
to wake up one morning
so far away from all the demands
and decisions which constantly
call out for answers I don't have,

and the next, to wake up
right back in the middle of it all.

I feel that there should be
a proper intermission –
some time to process
the weight and the beauty,
to absorb what I can't express.

T. Jason Vanderlaan

I'd rather have weeks at sea
with the wind sometimes assisting,
sometimes resisting my return,
while the waves comply with their whims
and I am forced to wrestle, to fight for balance

while I stare over the edge, looking ahead
through barriers of rain and fog and sun,
pondering the metaphor of travel
and trying to adjust to the change I feel inside.

Water

Growing Older, Perhaps Even Wiser

Everyday, I *know*
less and less.

44

T. Jason Vanderlaan

When the Sky Weeps

As I approached the post office counter, Joe looked up from a magazine he'd been reading. He smiled through his shaggy grey beard and mustache.

"Good evening. How's it going?"

Poor old guy. He obviously didn't know and I didn't have the heart to break the news to him tonight. He would find out soon enough; surely before I saw him next at church in a few days.

I replied with a simple, "Hey, how's it going Joe?" It was more of a greeting than a question and my response seemed to satisfy him.

I put my package on the counter and handed him a couple dollars. He punched a few buttons on the cash register and returned my change. Before I had a chance to leave, he spoke again.

"Hey, did you know that there are three ways we cry?"

I raised a quizzical eyebrow at him. He held up his magazine in response.

"It says it right here. Well, actually it says we have three types of tears."

I shifted uneasily. It appeared as if I was in for a science lesson before I could leave. I was tired and not in the mood. But he continued.

"The first type is always on our eyes. We don't actually cry these tears, but they help keep our eyes moist."

Is there a point to all this? Joe tended to ramble on about the strangest things sometimes. I tried to be polite and hoped my irritation wasn't showing.

"But then there are two types of tears that we cry: emotional and irritant. We have 'emotional tears' when we are sad or happy. The other kind are called 'irritant tears' and are produced when something gets in our eye that shouldn't be there. Those tears help protect us by washing away things that would bring harm to our eyes. Isn't that interesting?"

He had my full attention by now. I'd been thinking all day about how the sky had been crying on my behalf. I hadn't considered what *kind* of tears it might be crying.

I said a silent prayer, thanking God for giving me the patience to hear him out.

"Yeah, you know what, that is really interesting. I'd never thought about that before. Thanks, Joe."

He seemed a bit surprised by my sudden enthusiasm.

"Sure man, no problem." He smiled. "Well, have a good evening. See you around."

"See you, Joe."

I didn't open my umbrella as I left the store. The falling rain felt good against my skin. I looked up into the sky and wondered what lay ahead.

Rescue

(To the tune of Gustav Mahler's *Symphony No. 5 in C Sharp Minor: IV. Adagietto*)

If rescue ever came, I always imagined
it would be in the form of a ship –
a small spot on the horizon
promising me an escape, a return to my journey.

But maybe,
maybe this is my escape.

Maybe my rescue is coconuts and mangos,
clumsily constructed shelters, people
who need me as much as I need them.

Maybe this island was my destiny,
my destination all along.

Maybe the shipwreck was my rescue.

Because every morning I wake up
and every evening I lay down,
and in between I can't help but feel
that this is all I've ever wanted.

T. Jason Vanderlaan

My Grecian Romance

Athens, city of the gods,
you have caused so many to fall
with your faith in deities
who shared your same vices.

But I came to see for myself,
to walk your shores and explore your ruins.
I listened to your Mediterranean breeze,
gazed upon your fiery Greek sunsets,

and found, unexpectedly,
that you had led me
out of this darkness,
back to the God you never understood.

Mystery

There is one God.
One, and He is three.

And we can attempt
the three-leaf clover, or
the water, vapor, and ice.
But in the end
we must conclude:

Mystery!

Oh great and glorious,
unfathomable mystery
of the infinite,
co-eternal Three!

May we take comfort
in ways so much higher
than our own.

T. Jason Vanderlaan

Tidal Words

Words splash across the page,
ocean waves coming to wash away
sandcastles never meant to stand,
coming to drown my sorrow,
to take what's written in the sand
and carry it away, down
to where the light can't reach.

Tides to pull my past
into the depths of the sea.

Tides to smooth the shore
where I danced with the devil.

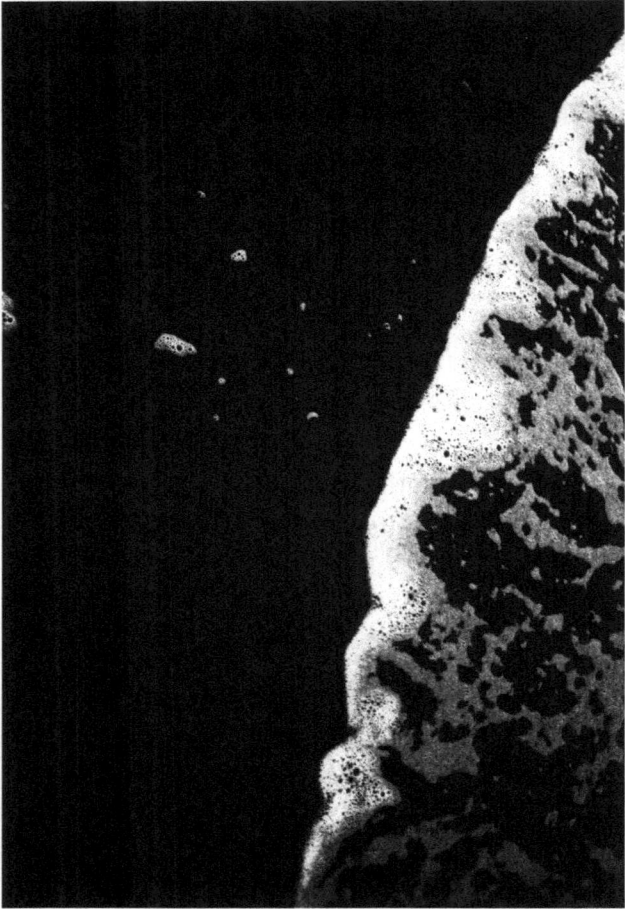

T. Jason Vanderlaan

Black Water

Let it come. I want this.

Why is it that when I look up and see heavy storm clouds rolling towards me, I feel... joy? A shiver runs through me; my heart is thrilled, not just because of their dark, majestic beauty, but because they *threaten* me.   I love the danger they foreshadow. I eagerly anticipate the wrath they promise.

And I have the perfect vantage point, standing atop the house I regret I've built.

No one is a wise builder from the start. At one point, we are all foolish builders, laying our foundations on shifting sands. Many realize, halfway through, the inevitable end. Others of us finish constructing not just houses, but mansions – investments that refuse to be ignored, refuse to be destroyed... at least not by the hand that built them.

Where then can I find an escape from these walls, from this prison I've created? Standing here, observing all I've spent myself for, I realize that what I really want, all I've ever wanted, is the aftermath of God's gracious devastation. I want to feel the sting of rain pounding against my face. I want the wind to rip across the sky, tearing at my hair and clothes. I want the thunder to shake the house beneath my feet and the bones beneath my skin. I want the lightning to burn the darkness from my eyes.

So let His righteous hand strike me – it will be an act of love. Let His rebuke fall heavily upon me – it is a blessing. Let me not refuse the rain that falls on the righteous and the unrighteous alike. Let it fall and lay waste to all I've built.

Let the storm clouds come. I need this.

T. Jason Vanderlaan

Dirty Water On Holy Hands

He washed my feet.

I, who misunderstood
like the other eleven.

I, who ate His mercy
and drank His forgiveness.

I, who deserted Him
like all the rest.

And I, who came back
to betray Him with a kiss.

He washed *my* feet.

Oasis for Flawed Souls

I've wandered these sands,
a donkey with no master,
a stranger in the wastelands,
wondering if there is meaning
in my wayward steps.

But today I thought I saw – though
maybe only a mirage – a vision:

One day soon a man will walk this way
and find life in my decay.

My jaw, now set so firm,
will yield to the hand of vengeance
as I become an instrument of justice
with the sweetest, severest melody.

And as the light fades,
the vultures will sing my song:
"Ramath lehi, elephiysh;
en hakkore, amuth batzama."

I take comfort in knowing
my bones will not bleach alone.

T. Jason Vanderlaan

Foreshadowing

The shadow-soaked figure
clutches the garden grass,
drenched with blood and water,
as the darkest demons
drape a shroud between the heavens
and His upturned eyes.

More alone
than any man has ever been,
He groans
and rises.

Years later, that moment
pierces the veil
and I receive the strength
to bear this weight
a little longer.

Buried, Part I

You can't tame the ocean. Try it sometime. One on one. You versus the waves. See how far you can go before you're forced to turn back. See how long you can stand against the breakers, their brutal force beating against you, pushing your feet back in the sand, back towards the shore.

And if you're feeling especially brave, try this at night. Keep pushing forward until you can't touch the bottom, until you sink beneath the waves. It is a thrilling, terrifying experience.

The ocean gives you two options: be tamed yourself by the very thing you seek to tame, or learn from the wildness of the waves and become like them.

When faced with the realization that you are not enough and will never be enough, you can either turn around and run, or you can take up the challenge to grow and learn from a power so much greater than yourself.

Let yourself be overwhelmed. Let yourself find strength in something stronger than yourself. Let yourself be buried beneath the power of the water, only to rise anew.

Shabbat Shalom

Peace truly is like a river: flowing,
though you don't always know where.
But it carries you along
if you surrender to the current,
as strong as it is gentle.

Or you can lay by the riverside, listening
to the poetry of water under a bridge
as you gaze up, watching the light fade
from the Friday evening sky, waiting
for the stars to come out and hint
at all the beauty that's yet to come.

T. Jason Vanderlaan

Twice Unlucky (Or, Two Wrongs Make a Rhombicuboctahedron)

I.
Every letter
will finally come to fruition
after all these years.

The page groans under the weight.

II.
Under the weight of these miles,
under this marathon sky,
I stagger forward,
rust in my joints,
over the frozen soil of Michigan –

the end not yet reached,
but no longer out of sight.

X.
Out of sight, my name is taken off the list.
No longer can I depend on the default.
From here on out, I have to want it.

From here on out, I have a choice.

XIII.
A choice can change everything,
even fate,
or at least that's what I'm hoping.

And so I choose.

I want Your name spread over me,
with all its glory unfurled in the wind.

I want it written on my heart,
no longer hearsay,
no longer an acquaintance.

I want the seeds buried deep;
I want to taste the coming harvest.

SpiritWater

You lead with footsteps
evident but unseen,
as water flows from rock
and waves part beneath my feet.

And You pursue –
quiet streams and stormy seas –
You walk on water, cross
over any distance
just to get to me.

So ask me for a drink,
because I am thirsty,

and though this well is deep,
I always come up short,
always come back empty again.

But You are
the never-ending source,
ever flowing, over flowing,
flooding my world
to bring life from death.

T. Jason Vanderlaan

The Truth About Authors

We are guilty, all of us,
poets and novelists alike,
of the half-finished,
half-dreamed, half-hearted.

We are guilt of the metaphor abandoned;
the idea discarded;
the story cut short;
the character half formed
in the womb of our imagination.

We, authors of plot lines and plot holes,
are guilty of abortions and murders,
of being distracted and bored and busy,
of leaving a man dangling on the edge of a cliff,
a woman waiting for her lover to return,
a simile unfinished, a rhyme without its other half.

And we,
we are so thankful
that God is not like us –

T. Jason Vanderlaan

so thankful that He is both
Author *and* Finisher,

that He not only writes our stories,
but became a character,

that He not only composes life's poetry,
but is the cadence in every word.

We are so thankful that He has promised
to finish what He began.

Water

T. Jason Vanderlaan

Acknowledgments (A Prayer of Thanks)

Jesus, I am so thankful for Your guidance in my life. Asaph's poetry in the Psalms resonates with my soul: "Your way led through the sea and Your path went through the stormy waters. Like a shepherd, You led your people, though Your footprints were unseen."

Whether in calm or chaos, I find comfort and courage in You, knowing that You have promised to work in every circumstance to bring out the best for all, even when I don't understand Your ways.

I also want to thank You for all the experiences, both easy and difficult, which have inspired this book. From my journeys in Japan and Greece to my time in Hawaii, Michigan, and this past summer in Ocean City, I am grateful for how You've used water to draw me closer to You.

I am also very thankful for the time and effort that Kayla McAuliffe, Matthew Lucio, and Beth-Anne White put into editing and refining this book. I am blessed to have such good friends and family.

About the Author

In *Fire*, the first book of the Elemental Endeavors series, T. Jason Vanderlaan explores our search for the source and fulfillment of our desires. We discover that some paths leave us cold, while others bring us closer to the fire of our truest longings. Amidst the chaos and uncertainty of our existence, we are continually led by a burning ache inside each of us, drawing us towards some unknown purpose.

Jason is also the author of *Unspoken Confessions,* a book that wrestles with the issues of sexual addiction, lust, dating (especially how men treat women), and purity. More than that, it is an attempt at honesty – we all struggle with flaws of our own and with receiving the grace of God.

Unspoken Confessions is a call to find light in the darkness and to allow God to create a new heart in us as we seek to develop healthy relationships.

Both books are available at:

balmandblade.com

Balm and Blade
Publishing

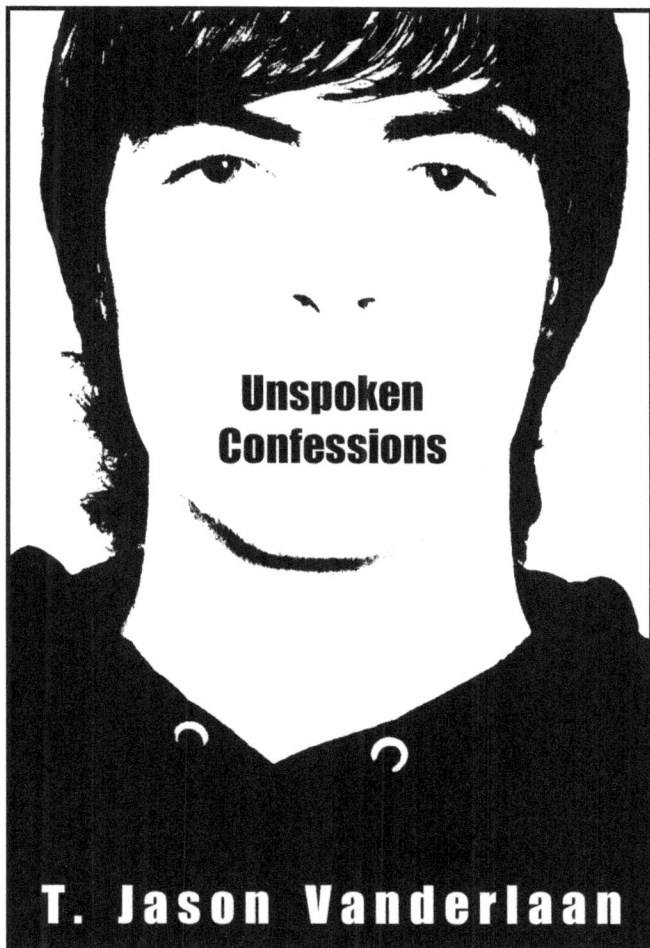

Unspoken
Confessions

T. Jason Vanderlaan

Also available from
Balm and Blade Publishing

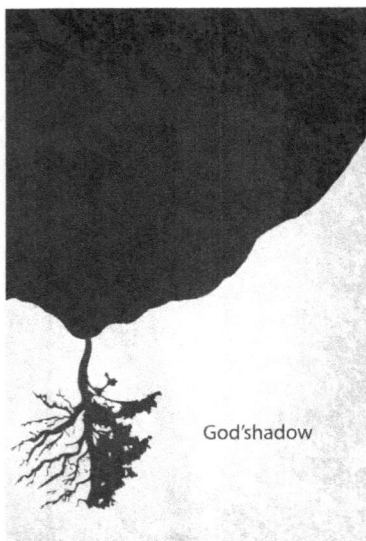

God'shadow

Daniel de Sevén takes us on journey deeper into doubt through a variety of creative essays meant to recall dormant doubts in the reader or else to create new ones. For many it will be an uncomfortable adventure but it is, the author argues, a necessary one because doubt is the delivery room of faith.

But be warned: this book isn't about the author trying to inductively prove a point. Rather, it is at once disjointed and communal, allowing readers to join the discussion and reach their own conclusions.

**For the latest news and updates
From Balm and Blade Publishing,**

**please visit us at:
balmandblade.com
facebook.com/balmandblade**

BALM AND BLADE
PUBLISHING

www.ingramcontent.com/pod-product-compliance
Lightning Source LLC
Chambersburg PA
CBHW070553030426
42337CB00016B/2482